D0105706

Macaws

By Erika and Jim Deiters

Raintree

ANIM
REST

www.raintreepublishers.co.uk

Visit our website to find out more information about Raintree books.

To order:
- ☎ Phone 44 (0) 1865 888112
- 🖹 Send a fax to 44 (0) 1865 314091
- 💻 Visit the Raintree Bookshop at www.raintreepublishers.co.uk to browse our catalogue and order online.

First published in Great Britain by Raintree Publishers, Halley Court, Jordan Hill, Oxford, OX2 8EJ, part of Harcourt Education.
Raintree is a registered trademark of Harcourt Education Ltd.

Originated by Dot Gradations
Printed and bound in China by South China Printing

ISBN 1 844 21115 0
07 06 05 04 03
10 9 8 7 6 5 4 3 2 1

British Library Cataloguing in Publication Data
Deiters, Erika & Jim
1. Macaws – Juvenile literature
2. Rainforest ecology – Juvenile literature
598.7'1
A catalogue for this book is available from the British Library.

Acknowledgements
The publishers would like to thank the following for permission to reproduce photographs:
Corbis/Michael & Patricia Fogden, p. **13**. Steve Kaufman, p. **15**. Ken Lucas, p. **24**. Parrot Jungle, pp. **1, 5, 6, 15, 19, 28–29**. Photo Network/Mark Newman, p. **8**. Photophile/Anthony Mercieca, p. **22**. Visuals Unlimited/Mary Morina, pp. **11, 26**; Barbara Magnuson, p. **16**; R.F. Ashley, p. **18**. Wildlife Conservation Society, p. **21**.

Cover photograph reproduced with permission of Corbis Royalty Free

Every effort has been made to contact copyright holders of any material reproduced in this book. Any omissions will be rectified in subsequent printings if notice is given to the publishers.

Contents

Any words appearing in the text in bold, **like this**, are explained in the Glossary.

USA

MEXICO

Caribbean Sea

GUATEMALA
BELIZE
HONDURAS
EL SALVADOR
NICARAGUA
COSTA RICA
PANAMA

VENEZUELA
GUYANA
SURINAM
FRENCH GUIANA

COLOMBIA

ECUADOR

Amazon River

PERU

BRAZIL

BOLIVIA

PARAGUAY

South Pacific Ocean

URUGUAY

CHILE

ARGENTINA

South Atlantic Ocean

North Atlantic Ocean

N
W   E
S

Range of the blue macaw
Surrounding land
Sea
Borders
Rivers

A quick look at macaws

What do macaws look like?

Macaws are large, colourful birds. Their feathers are usually green, blue, red or yellow. They have short necks and large rounded heads. They have thick, curved beaks and very long tails.

Where do macaws live?

Some macaws live in the rainforests of Mexico and Central and South America. They also live on islands off the coast of South America.

What do macaws eat?

Macaws eat nuts, berries, leaves and buds. A bud is the part of a plant that grows into a leaf or flower. Macaws also eat food that other animals will not touch. They eat fruit that is not ripe. They even eat foods containing toxins, or poisons, that would make other animals ill.

Macaws are colourful parrots that live in rainforest trees.

Macaws in the rainforest

Some kinds of macaws live in rainforests. Rainforests are places where many different trees and plants grow close together. A lot of rain falls in rainforests.

Macaws are the largest and most colourful members of the parrot family. The scientific name for this family is Psittacidae. It means 'to repeat something'. Parrots are known for repeating sounds that they hear.

Macaws are named after the macaw palm tree. The birds eat the nuts from this tree.

There are about 300 kinds of parrots. Their bright colours and voices have made them some of the best-known birds in the world. Other members of the parrot family include parakeets and cockatoos.

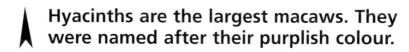 Hyacinths are the largest macaws. They were named after their purplish colour.

Kinds of macaws

Scientists think there are seventeen macaw species. A species is a group of animals or plants that are closely related to each other. Examples of rainforest macaws are the green-winged macaw, the chestnut-fronted macaw, Buffon's macaw and the blue-and-yellow macaw.

Blue-and-yellow macaws are large birds. They grow up to 84 centimetres long. They are blue on top and yellow underneath, with black beaks. They live in the South American rainforests from Panama south to Brazil, Paraguay and Bolivia. They like to nest in dead trees and are not in great danger of dying out.

Buffon's macaws are also called great green macaws. They grow up to 86 centimetres long. They are green with a red forehead. They live in the rainforests of Central America and Colombia and Ecuador in South America.

The largest macaws are the hyacinth macaws. They grow up to 102 centimetres long. They are deep blue with yellow patches around their eyes. They live in trees near the grasslands of Brazil, the largest country in South America. Only about 3000 remain in the wild. They live in both rainforests and drier areas.

The smallest macaws are the red-shouldered macaws. They are about 30 centimetres long. Like all macaws, they have long tails. They prefer to live in the drier areas of north-eastern South America than in rainforests.

Range and habitat

Many macaws live in the rainforests of Mexico and Central and South America. Roughly twelve species live in the rainforests of Brazil. Others live on islands off the coast of South America.

Like most birds, macaws live in trees. Macaws can live in many places, including river valleys, swamps, grasslands and mountain rainforests. Some species like the warmth of tropical areas. These are hot and rainy areas of the world.

Appearance

Macaws are large. They can be many colours, including green, blue, red and yellow. Unlike many birds, both males and females are colourful. They have short necks, large heads and very long tails. Macaws also have thick, curved beaks. The beaks of larger macaws are strong enough to snap a broomstick. They use their beaks like people use their hands. They can hold their food or comb each other's feathers with their beaks.

Some macaws have **cheek patches** near their eyes. These patches often have patterns of small feathers. The patches turn pink when macaws

This macaw is using its feet to hold food while it eats.

are angry, nervous or excited. The patches are like a person's fingerprints. No two are alike.

Macaws have four toes on each of their feet. Two toes point forwards. The other two point backwards. This gives macaws a strong grip. They use their feet to hold food and to grab branches. Like people, macaws are left-handed or right-handed. Most macaws are left-handed.

These macaws are eating clay from a river bank.

What macaws eat

Macaws eat nuts, berries, leaves and seeds. They can crack open hard nutshells with their strong jaws and beaks. They have the strongest bite of any bird. They use their tongues to dig inside shells to get nuts.

Macaws eat seeds containing toxins, or poisons, from mahogany and soapbox, or sandbox, trees. These seeds would make many animals ill, but not macaws. Macaws can eat them because they also eat clay from river banks. Macaws visit clay mounds about three times a week. They cling to the clay and scrape chunks into their mouths. If the macaws did not eat the clay, the toxins from the seeds would stay in their bodies. The clay traps the toxins. Then the clay and the toxins pass out in the form of **waste**. This prevents macaws from getting ill.

This macaw is eating fruit from a papaya tree.

Do you know why macaws land in palm trees? The trees have smooth trunks. This helps protect them from some predators. Reptiles and cats cannot climb the smooth trees.

How macaws digest food

Macaws also eat unripe fruit. They like the seeds inside the fruit. Unripe fruit and hard nuts take a long time to digest. Digest means to break down food so the body can use it.

There are small stones in the clay macaws eat. The stones collect in a part of the body called a **gizzard**. These stones help grind up the food macaws eat. This helps the birds digest their food.

How macaws find food

Rainforest trees can grow more than 30 metres tall. In a rainforest, the area of thick leaves and branches high above the ground is called the **canopy**. The canopy has lower, middle and upper parts. Macaws use their good eyesight to find nuts and fruit in the canopy.

These two macaws are cleaning each other's feathers.

A macaw's life cycle

Wild macaws can live to be 45 years old. In zoos, these birds can live longer than many humans. They may live to be 70 years old.

Macaws begin to mate when they are about five years old. Like most parrots, macaws stay with the same mate for life. The male and female clean each other's feathers. They touch each other's beaks. They fly so close to each other that their wings almost touch.

Not all female macaws lay eggs every year. When they do lay eggs, most females lay only two eggs at a time per year. Sometimes these eggs do not hatch. If both eggs hatch, usually only one chick lives to be an adult. The parents feed only one bird. It is either the first chick that hatches or the larger chick.

This female parrot is sitting on eggs in her nest.

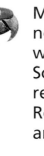

Macaws may have lived as far north as Arizona, in the south-western part of the USA. Scientists have found the remains of scarlet macaws there. Remains are what is left of an animal after it dies.

A macaw's nest

Usually, a pair of male and female macaws builds a nest far from other macaws. They make a nest in the hole of a dead tree. They put bark and twigs in the bottom of the hole. As soon as the female lays her eggs, the pair stops being **social**. This means the birds stop living in a group of birds. The pair must make sure that other birds do not take over the nest.

Females sit on their eggs for 12 to 35 days. During this time, the male hunts for food. He stores food in a pouch in his throat. He brings it back to the nest to share with the female. When the eggs hatch, both parents take turns hunting for food and feeding the young.

Young

Macaws take care of their chicks for about one year. Chicks are born blind. Their eyes open after nine to sixteen days. Chicks are born without feathers. Fluffy feathers appear in about eight days. These feathers are called **down** feathers. They are only for warmth. They are not used for flying.

Chicks are not very active. They eat, sleep and grow. They beg for food by flapping their wings and screeching. They take partly digested fruit and nuts from their parents' mouths. They live in their nests for two to four months. Once they begin to fly, young macaws are called **fledglings**.

Young macaws are in danger from predators. Reptiles, climbing cats, eagles and other predators attack young macaws when they are in their nests.

This is a young macaw. It is weak and unable to defend itself against predators.

Macaws are social. The birds usually fly together in groups.

A macaw's day

Macaws are very social birds. They like to spend time together. Sometimes there are as many as a hundred in a group. They make small clicking sounds to say hello to each other. They are quiet only when they eat or sleep. High in the canopy, macaws are safe from many enemies. The leaves there provide a place to hide from predators. Predators are animals that hunt other animals and eat them. Reptiles and climbing cats are predators that hunt macaws. However, the predators cannot climb high in the canopy. They can catch only the macaws that come close to the forest floor. But even high in the treetops, macaws are not always safe. Harpy eagles hunt them there.

Macaws do not travel far from home. They usually fly to the same area every day. They visit the same trees to look for nuts and fruit.

Macaws rest in the shade during hot afternoons. They use their beaks to pick out dead feathers and parasites. A parasite, such as a tick, is an animal or plant that lives on or inside another living thing.

At night, **flocks** of macaws meet at a **sleeping tree**. Most sleeping trees are taller than the trees and bushes around them. They are usually dead trees with no leaves. Macaws argue with each other for the best sleeping spots. In time, they find a good place to spend the night. Sleeping trees have no leaves so predators have nowhere to hide. This helps keep macaws safe at night.

Most macaws are endangered because of the loss of their rainforest habitat.

How are macaws doing?

Most macaw species are either threatened or endangered. This means they are in danger of becoming **extinct**. The red Cuban macaw is already extinct. The glaucous macaw may also be extinct.

People are one of the biggest dangers to macaws. They cut down trees in the rainforests to raise and feed cattle. The macaws need these trees for nesting, for finding food and for sleeping. In the last 100 years, over half of the world's rainforests have been destroyed.

People have even been known to use colourful macaw feathers to make special clothing.

Macaws will die without rainforest trees to live in.

Protecting macaws

Some people take young macaws from their nests and sell them as pets. Macaws taken from the wild do not make good pets. Many die when they are moved from their habitat. A habitat is a place where an animal or plant naturally lives. Macaws taken from their natural home can easily catch diseases or die from stress caused by the change in habitat. Today, laws protect wild macaws. It is against the law to take these birds from their habitats.

Scientists have made macaw **reserves**. A reserve is a place where animals are protected. Macaws are safe in the reserves. When macaws in a refuge lose feathers, scientists collect them. They give the feathers to people who use them for clothing. That way people do not take macaws from the wild.

Many people understand that macaws are important to life in the rainforests. They must teach other people what they know. Together, people of all ages can help keep macaws alive in their rainforest homes for a very long time.

colourful feathers
see pages 5, 7, 10

long tail
see pages 5, 9, 10

eyes
see pages 15, 20

powerful beak
see pages 5, 9, 10, 13

feet
see page 11

Glossary

canopy thick area of leaves and branches high up in the treetops

cheek patch special area near a macaw's eye that goes pink when the bird is angry, nervous, or excited

down soft body feathers of a young bird

endangered in danger of dying out

extinct species that has died out forever

fledgling young bird

flock group of animals of one kind that live, travel and feed together

gizzard muscular part of a bird's stomach where food is ground up

reserve place where living things are protected or sheltered

sleeping tree special tree where birds spend the night

social living mainly in groups

waste undigested food that leaves an animal's body in droppings

Internet sites

Macaw Landing Foundation
www.MacawLanding.org

Rainforest Concern
www.rainforestconcern.org

World Wide Fund for Nature (WWF)
www.panda.org

Useful address

WWF – UK
Panda House, Weyside Park
Godalming, Surrey
GU7 1XR

Book to read

Theodorou, R, Telford, C. *Amazing Journeys:*
Up a Rainforest Tree. Heinemann Library,
Oxford, 1998

Index